Young Learner's

Look-n-Colour ANIMALS AND BIRDS

ANIMALS

COW

GOAT

CAT

DOG

HORSE

DONKEY

CAMEL

PANDA

ELEPHANT

GIRAFFE

BEAR

LION

LEOPARD

TIGER

WOLF

FOX

DEER

KANGAROO

MONKEY

ORANGUTAN

HIPPOPOTAMUS

CROCODILE

RHINOCEROS

SNAKE

BIRDS

PIGEON

SPARROW

PARROT

GOLDFINCH

MOCKINGBIRD

CARDINAL

LORIKEET

MACAW

HUMMINGBIRD

ROBIN

PEACOCK

PHEASANT

PELICAN

WOODPECKER

OWL

TURKEY

EAGLE

BUNTING

VULTURE

ROOSTER

BLUE JAY

BLUE BIRD